BACKYARD BIRDS

EAST

GULF OF ALASKA

Hudson Bay

PACIFIC OCEAN

ATLANTIC OCEAN

GULF OF MEXICO

GULF OF CALIFORNIA

This books covers a selection of common species found in backyards in the eastern and midwestern United States and Canada.

BACKYARD BIRDS
EAST

A SEYMORE GULLS FIELD GUIDE
PHOTOS BY BRIAN E. SMALL

Scott & Nix, Inc.

NEW YORK

PUBLISHED BY
SCOTT & NIX, INC.
150 W 28TH ST, STE 1900
NEW YORK, NY 10001
SCOTTANDNIX.COM

FIRST EDITION 2023

ISBN 978-1-935622-77-2

SCOTT & NIX, INC. BOOKS ARE DISTRIBUTED TO THE TRADE BY
INDEPENDENT PUBLISHERS GROUP (IPG)
814 NORTH FRANKLIN STREET
CHICAGO, IL 60610
800-888-4741
IPGBOOK.COM

THE PAPER OF THIS BOOK IS FSC CERTIFIED, WHICH ASSURES
IT WAS MADE FROM WELL MANAGED FORESTS AND OTHER
CONTROLLED SOURCES.

PRINTED IN CHINA THROUGH PORTER PRINT GROUP, BETHESDA, MARYLAND

CONTENTS

6 A NOTE FROM SEYMORE GULLS

7 PARTS OF A BIRD

8 BACKYARD BIRDS

132 DEDICATION

133 ABOUT THE AUTHOR AND PHOTOGRAPHER

134 INDEX

I know it's crazy to write another bird book when there are already so many great guides out there. But, I'll do almost anything to get more people interested in looking at these wonderful little dinosaurs. And besides, I really wanted to "keep it simple" and "keep it fun." So, I present to you, *Backyard Birds East: A Seymore Gulls Bird Guide.* It's for those of us that love big pictures and just a little bit of text. A guide with the lowest barrier to entry possible. A book for literally everyone at every age who thinks a picture is worth a thousand words, and the words are worth like maybe fifteen words.

The goal is to make birding accessible. Knowing a creature's name is a powerful thing, and discovering the diversity in your backyard is one of the first steps to helping embrace our feathered friends (and their homes and foods) and welcoming them to our yards.

I've included 99-plus birds in this guide that are common in neighborhoods across the eastern USA and Canada (east of the Rocky Mountains). Not every yard is the same, of course, so if you see other types of birds that might not be in this guide, go online or go look at a more complete guide and find that bird! You'll be happy you did.

This book is a love letter to our adorable/cute/incredible/wonderful backyard birds. I hope once you start to learn about them, you don't stop there. This is just a jumping-off point. Next is joining a local birding group, planting a native plant to attract a hummingbird, learning about different ways to help increase biodiversity in our neighborhoods, and venturing out past yards and into parks on the search for more wonders of nature.

I'm so happy you picked this book up, and I can't wait for you to keep progressing on your journey! Start a list of the birds you've seen. Share your bird anecdotes with friends, don't stop talking about them at parties, send bird memes and photos to internet personalities (info@pdxbirder.com), and just enjoy the whole process that is birdwatching.

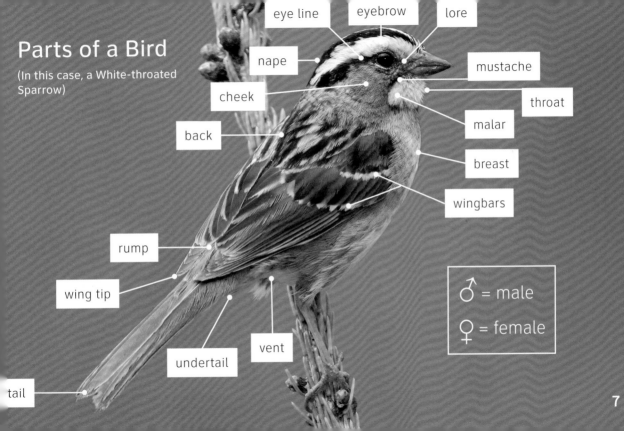

Parts of a Bird

(In this case, a White-throated Sparrow)

eye line

eyebrow

lore

nape

mustache

cheek

throat

malar

back

breast

wingbars

rump

wing tip

♂ = male

♀ = female

undertail

vent

tail

Mourning Dove

blue eye-ring

thin bill

black dots

slender

"coo-ooooo"

long pointy tail

widespread neighborhood & grassland dove

8

Eurasian Collared-Dove

dark primaries

dark collar

short tail

pale gray overall

chunky

daytime hooter

devours millet & grains

introduced in 1970s

Rock Pigeon
(feral)

iridescent nape

super variable plumage

plump

majestic urban mascot

Domesticated
5,000 years ago!

10

Chimney Swift

long curved wings

stiff wingbeats

tiny tail

cigar shaped body

erratic aerial insectivore

urban chimney nester

11

Ruby-throated Hummingbird

♂

Ruby!

greenish sides

only common "hummer" in East & Midwest

weighs less than a nickel

males compete for territory especially at feeders

♀

plain
white
throat

teeny tiny feet

Hummingbird nectar recipe
• 1 part sugar
• 4 parts water
• no dyes
Clean often!

attracted to red flowers—trumpet creeper,
beebalm, trumpet honeysuckle, & cardinal flower

Cooper's Hawk (adult)

bug-eyed

dark cap

stern look

light nape

steely blue back

dense orange barring

white undertail coverts

crow-sized yard predator

head out past wings

neck

(juvenile a.k.a. "juvie")

t-shape in flight

long tail

glides w/ slow, countable wingbeats

15

small, round head

dark cap extends down nape

barrel chested

little accipiter

preys on sparrow-sized birds

no neck

Sharp-shinned Hawk

(adult)

square tail w/ little

head barely pokes out past wrists

stubby, roundish wings

(juvie)

shorter, boxy tail

heavily streaked chest

quick wingbeats in straight flight

17

common neighborhood drummer

mustachioed ♂

black bib

spotted tummy

yellow under tail & wing

white rump in flight

barred wings

Northern Flicker

♀ lacks mustache

Red-headed Woodpecker

white front

found in older
suburbs &
open pine forests

Red!

black
back

hides
snacks
for
later

black
wingtips

19

bill half
length
of head

♂ w/
red spot

"Pik!"

black sides & tail

2" smaller than
Hairy Woodpecker

tiny nieghborhood
woodpecker

♀ lacks

Downy Woodpecker

mostly found on trunks & large branches

bill same length as head

mostly black back w/ speckled feathers

"Speak!"

mature forest woodpecker

Hairy Woodpecker

Red-bellied Woodpecker

barely red belly

light chest

red cap

uniformly zebra striped

attract w/ suet & peanuts

♂ w/ red forehead & chin

hint of yellow

winter in Southeast & breed in Northeast

white nape

white shoulder

Yellow-bellied Sapsucker

drills sap wells in tree trunks

23

Pileated Woodpecker

♂ w/ red mustache

♀ w/ black mustache

red crest

HUGE! (crow-sized)

black body

our largest woodpecker

Eastern Kingbird

big noggin

black uppers

white unders

white tail tip

loves a conspicuous perch

takes large insects in flight

25

Eastern Wood-pewee

peaked head

bicolored- bill

bold wingbars

gray vest

found in wooded areas & tree canopies

doesn't wag tail

"peee-a-weeeee"

migrant tyrant flycatcher—here from May–Oct

Eastern Phoebe

darkest on crown

thin black bill

faint wingbars

broad white chest

active tail wagger

yellow washed tummy

"Fee-bee!"

bold little mealworm lovers

wetland adjacent flycatcher

Great Crested Flycatcher

great crest

chunky bill

gray chin

reddish brown wings & back

yellow tummy

long body & tail

loud but secretive— yells "wheep!" from the canopies

Blue-headed Vireo

bluish-headed

bespectacled

yellow armpits

white unders

winters along Gulf & breeds in Appalachia & NE

methodical branch hopper

flocks w/ warblers & chickadees

29

White-eyed Vireo

gray head

white eye

yellow lores

gray tummy

found in super dense low shrubbery; easier to hear than see

vireos sing repetitive songs

Red-eyed Vireo

crisp eyebrow

red eye

gray/green back

serious expression

white unders

nests high in deciduous trees

sings short repetitive song **thousands** of times a day

American Crow

slim, straightish bill

smooth throat feathers

"Caw! Caw!"

crow-sized

does a lot of flapping, not much soaring

flat-edged tail

loves unsalted peanuts   neighborhood corvid

Common Raven

thick, curved bill

soars & does acrobatics

shaggy neck beard

"Groak! Groak!"

twice the size of a crow

solitary omnivore

wedge-shaped tail

Blue Jay

adjustable crest

intricate blue patterning

necklace

white unders

love acorns

Super smart!

unmistakeable & unignorable

34

Tufted Titmouse

Tuft!

large eyes

lovable face

dark gray back

light unders

peachy flank

tame feeder friend

Black-capped Chickadee

black cap

bright white in wings

scraggly line between black chin & white chest

"chicka-deee-deee-deee-deee[

slightly larger, slightly more vibrant chickadee

Carolina Chickadee

white cheek

grayish white in wings

little bill

tiny

black chin

clean line between
black chin & white chest

Brown Creeper

Creeps!

light eyebrow

brown speckled back

white unders

"Trees, trees , beautiful trees"

flies to base of tree &
creeps up in search of
insects

Red-breasted Nuthatch

gray back

white eyebrow

black eye-stripe

conifer excavator

"Yank! Yank! Yank!"

female's belly lighter than male's

White-breasted Nuthatch

dark crown stripe

chisel bil

"Mew! Mew!"

white face & tummy

deciduous forest
descender

attract w/ sunflower
seeds

Brown-headed Nuthatch

gray back & sides

Brown!

white chin

found in family groups &
mixed winter flocks

tiny nut-
hatch of
SE pine
forests

Barn Swallow

blue cap & back

rusty forehead & throat

classic bird tattoo

long forked tail

makes cup nests from mouthfuls of mud

Tree Swallow

metalic blue-green

dark eye-mask

white stops below eye

oves fields & wetlands

Attract to your yard w/ nest boxes

Purple Martin

♂ adult

all dark wings & tummy

techno-sounding calls

nests in woodpecker holes & manmade bird condos

The big purple one!

large, long wings

♀ /immature male

light collar & forehead

dark wings & back

light tummy

our largest swallow

45

Ruby-crowned Kinglet

crisp yellow on black

thin bill

yellow feet

hyperactive shrub forager

pops crown
when excite

Golden-crowned Kinglet

gold & black crown

white eyebrow

dark around eyes

yellowish back

mixed-flock chickadee friend

high-canopy conifer kinglet

Winter Wren

tail popped

mousy size
mousy color
mousy lifestyle

speckled tummy
& wings

denizen of the forest floor

House Wren

faint eyebrow

bicolor bill

genrally brown & plain

tail unpopped

migrant wren: winters in Gulf States breeds TN & north

loves brushy yards; nests in manmade nooks

49

Carolina Wren

clean white eyebrow

jaunty tail

curved bill

sweet potato

boisterous singer

warm buffy unders

attract w/ dense shru
& suet feeder

European Starling

shaggy

yellow bill

irridescent purple & green

mimics other
bird calls

aby bird

murmuration
flocker

Northern Mockingbird

jay-sized

territorial neighborhood mimic

dark wings & tail

loves a manmade perch (chimney, mailbox, powerline, etc.)

during breeding season even sings at night

white wing patches

Gray Catbird

dark cap

gray

raspy "meow" call

rusty undertail

secretive, hides in low dense bushes

53

Brown Thrasher

yellow eye

barred wings

long tail

striped

attract w/
dense brush &
native berries

loves to thrash
(kick up leaf litter
to find insects)

Cedar Waxwing

mullet

silky browns & yellows

black mask

waxy red wingtips

eats berries & bugs

yellow tail

55

American Robin

dark head & back

white face patterning

yellow bill

orange tummy

our most
common
thrush

Baby
bird!

Eastern Bluebird

Blue!

all blue wings

orange throat & breast

♂ more saturated color than ♀

white belly

attract w/ nest boxes & meal worms

Wood Thrush

unbarred wings

neon brown head

big eye w/ eyering

migratory,
here Apr–Oct

boldest of spots

58

leaf litter lover

Hermit Thrush

thin, white eyering

gray-brown back

usty wing-edge

rusty tail

white breast w/ dark spots

most commonly found in winter

furtive forest-floor forager

House Sparrow

gray crown

black face & throat

rufous nape & back

light gray cheek

♂

noisy

Old World sparrow
of parking lots

light eyebrow

striped back

♀/immature male

gray-brown unders

competes w/ natives for nest boxes

House Finch

brightest on forehead

pale cheek

top of bill curves downward

plumage ranges from red to yellow

♂

streaked sides

bright rump

ubiquitous feeder finch

plain face & cheek

♀/immature male

long, blurry brown
streaking

long tail

forms large, sunflower
seed-eating flocks

63

Purple Finch

overall raspberry coloration

red forehead & cheek

♂

warbles from tree-tops in spring

clean, unstreaked look

white tummy

white eyebrow

dark cheek patch

♀/immature male

thick triangle bill

short streaks

found year-round north of PA
& winters everywhere but south FL

65

American Goldfinch

black forehead

Yellow!

orange bill

♂ breeding plumage

black wings w/ white bars

flight call: "Po-ta-to-chip"

attract w/ sunflower & thistle

♂ & ♀ fully molt into sensible winter plumage

yellowish face

yellow-brown back

black wings w/ pale wingbars

unstreaked tummy

loves seedheads
& unmown yards

67

Common Redpoll

red forehead

dark face

adorable triangle bill

pink wash

streaked front

loves birch trees

tiny winter resident alon
the Canada border

Evening Grosbeak

♂

black & white wings

yellow brow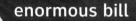

enormous bill

lemony tummy

♀

Irruptive finch: found along Canada border though some winters will descend south in search of food.

Pine Siskin

cheek & eyebrow
same color

pointy bill

streaky back

yellow in wings & tail

call "rising zipper"

short notched tail

Irruptive nomadic finch: mostly found in winter but it's abundan & range are unpredictable as flocks roam in search of food.

Savannah Sparrow

yellow lores

light bill

fine streaking

white tummy

short tail

Quintisential grassland songbird: there are 17 subspecies of Savannah sparrow, so expect variability in appearance.

Chipping Sparrow

(non-breeding plumage)

redish cap

rusty face

dark eyeline

white throat

plain gray tummy

Forms large winter flocks. Winter in FL & s. TX; in summer found in grass forests & parks across the US.

bright red cap

(breeding plumage)

thin black eyeline

white eyebrow

clean gray unders

Nests in woodlots, parks & gardens; attract w/ sunflower seeds.

"juvie"

Field Sparrow

cap & cheek same color

white eyering

pink bill

red shoulders & back

no dot

year-round
field resident

American Tree Sparrow

rufous crowned

bicolor bill

eyeline goes
through eye

double white wingbars

dot

clean unders

winter resident
& Arctic breeder

White-crowned Sparrow

black & white crown

eye stripe

yellow-orange bill

gray cheeks

gray tummy

attract w/ seeds in a tray feeder

1st winter

White-throated Sparrow

crisp black & white crown

yellow! lores

russety back

stunning white throat

our most common flocking winter sparrow

tan "morph"

Fox Sparrow

unstreaked head

gray head & neck

solid reddish rump

triangular tummy spots

winter hedgerow visitor

78

Song Sparrow

stripy head

gray bill

stripy back

stripy shoulders

stripy front

Stripy (& probably in your yard right now)!

Eastern Towhee

black head & chest

red eye

white outer tail

rufous sides

white tummy

ground scratching thicket skulker

Big!
(for a sparrow)

Dark-eyed Junco

beady black eye

pinkish bill

slatey top half

white bottom half

winter feeder visitor

white outer tail

Red-winged Blackbird

red & yellow shoulder patch

downcurved bill

loud distinct song
"Jus-Tin Beee-Be

♂

black body

loves sunflowers & bird feeders

light eyebrow

pointy bill

found near wetlands

♀ (that's right)

rufous edged feathers

dense streaking

often feeds w/ sparrow flocks but its the big one of the group

winner of the most misidentified bird award

Brown-headed Cowbird

matte brown head

big cone bill

♂

chunky

iridescent
black body

joins large mixed
blackbird flocks

short tail

upturned head

thick base of bill

pale throat

uniformly brown

♀

"brood parasite"—lays eggs in other birds' nests

85

Bobolink

yellow nape

white back

black front

loves grains & bugs

grassland breeder threated by habitat loss; travel up to 12,000 miles from Paraguay to breed in NE

nonbreeding

Common Grackle

yellow eye

long bill

bronzy body

purple & green
iridescence

Enjoys a good bath!

Boat-tailed Grackle

light eye

♂

purple & blue iridescence

huge keel-shaped tail
(as long as their body)

long
thin
legs

♀

larger than
Common Grackles

warm brown
head & unders

long tail

long & skinny

doesn't stray far from saltwater habitats; mostly
coastal Gulf of TX to FL & up to Long Island

Eastern Meadowlark

grass camoflauge

yellow tummy & breast

hides in fields & sings
from fenceposts

beautiful variable
song

Baltimore Oriole

black head & back

vibrant orange
(unmistakeble)

weave intricate
hanging nests

orange
outer
tail

attract w/ citrus & big deciduous trees

Orchard Oriole

black head

bluish bill

black throat

attract w/ mulberry & orange slices

(2nd year ♂)

chestnut-orange distinctive

all black tail

(hatch year

olive/brown back

short bill

♀

Tail wagger

lemony yellow

our smallest oriole (but larger than any warbler)

Yellow-rumped Warbler

black mask

gray back

white chin

breeding ♂

"butter butt"

yellow armpits

our winter warbler—
attract w/ suet feeder

white eye-arcs

dark cheek

breeding ♀

all have yellow rump

yellow

often seen catching
flying insects

95

Pine Warbler

greenish yellow head

♂

clean yellow throat

2 wingbars

yellow body

white vent

loves pine trees &
eat seeds at feeders

♀/immature male

white eye arcs

largish bill

2 wingbars

yellow wash

pretty big (for a warbler)

ear-round resident LA to
A—breeds north to Canada

Yellow Warbler

black & yellow wings

Bright yellow!

♂

stout bill

rusty streaking

clean yellow
unders

♀

found low in brushy areas next to water

neotropical migrant; widespread from Apr–Oct

Common Yellowthroat

black mask

♂

Yellow throat!

"witchity witchity witchity"

yellow
undertail

really are pretty "common"
near marshes, wetlands, &
brushy fields

brown back & face

yellow undertail

gray cheek

♀

forages low & hides
in tall grass

Orange-crowned Warbler

breeding adult

gray back

white eye arcs

needly bill

yellow wash

winters from TX–NC; seen north on migration to Canada

Northern Parula

white eye arcs

yellow back

2 white wingbars

yellow throat & chest

Gorgeous!

flits around quickly to catch insects & spiders

Yellow-throated Warbler

gray back & cap

white eyebrow

black malar stripes

Yellow!

treetop forager

breeds in mature forest
& swamps

104

Black-and-white Warbler

stripy head

white eyebrow

♀ w/ white throat ♂

w/ black throat

forages near tree trunks like a nuthatch

tail popped
& fanned

American Redstart

black back & head

♂

yellow-
orange outer
tailfeathers

orange accents

white tummy

active understory insect hunter

flashes outer tailfeathers to flush prey

gray head

♀

yellow armpits

white unders

builds nests in parks & woodlots

Magnolia Warbler

black mask

yellow chin

black throat

bold white wing patch

♂

white wingbars

gray head

streaky-ish unders

♀

hrub forager & NE breeder

109

Chestnut-sided Warbler

yellow wingbar

yellow cap

♂

black mask

Chestnut!

tail popped

breeds in Appalachia & north to ME & Great Lakes

♀

pale bill

patchy chestnut

feeds & nests in dense shrubs

Prothonatory Warbler

formerly known
as the "Golden Swamp Warbler"

golden head

olive back

blue tail & wings

cavity nester; will
sometimes use nes
boxes

little orb of
sunshine

Black-throated Green Warbler

greenish back

thick white
wingbars

streaked armpits

bright yellow
eyebrow (& face)

Black!

high-canopy
warbling songster

♀

white
throat

Prairie Warbler ♂

red streaking

yellow eyebrow

black streaking

yellow unders

hunts low to ground & deep in bushes

114

♀ /immature male

gray cheek

non-stop tail wagger

yellow belly

winters in FL breeds north up to New England

Blackburnian Warbler ♂

black back

black mask

fiery orange

bold white
wing patch

often seen bug hunting
in the treetops

♀/immature male

double white wingbars

light eyebrow

dark gray cheek

yellow wash

breeds in conifers from GA
Appalachias north to Canada

Summer Tanager

lil' crest

big bill

sometimes orange

♂

red w/ red wings

long tail

drab back

♀

golden yellows

flycatcher & fruit plucker

119

Scarlet Tanager

red w/ black wings

♂

smaller
grayish bill

dark shoulders

Scarlet!

citrusy yellows

contrasting
dark wings

♀

short tail

nests in NE forests

121

Northern Cardinal

crested

big red bill

♂

black

It's the year-round red one!

Cardinalis cardinalis—so nice they named it twice!

red crest

♀

thick, orange,
triangular bill

one of few female
birds to sing

red accents

loves sunflower seeds

Rose-breasted Grosbeak

b&w wings

Wow!
wonderfully
unmistakable

♂

vibrant
rosy red

crisp
white

neotropical migrant;
here Apr–Oct

attract w/ sunflower seeds & native fruit trees

pale eyebrow

huge pink bill

♀

stripy white unders

125

Blue Grosbeak

Blue!

black lores

breeding ♂

silver bill

rusty wingbars

breeds in
shrubby fields

tail often fanned

darker head

massive bill

♀ /immature male

2 cinnamon wingbars

tawny body

twice as large as
Indigo Bunting

127

Indigo Bunting

breeding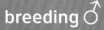

indigo head

small bil

turquoise body

black wingtips

loves a weedy field

♀/immature male

hint of blue

light throat

light streaking

dark tail

attract w/ meal worms or small seeds

light tummy

Painted Bunting

adult ♂

dazzling combo of strawberry, lime green, & cerulean blue

as shy as it is spectacular

♀/immature male

yellow eyering

green tail & back

yellow unders

attract w/
millet feeder &
dense bush for
hiding

131

DEDICATION

To my daughter Margo and all future birdwatchers,
may this book inspire a lifelong love for birds, while
reminding us to do our best to conserve their
habitats for the enjoyment of all.

SEYMORE GULLS, a.k.a. Eric Carlson, is a Portland, Oregon based bird enthusiast. He creates books and videos to educate his audience and inspire a love of birds. Seymore also leads weekly beginner bird walks where he shares his binoculars and knowledge with all who attend. He believes that birding can change the world and it's his personal mission to get as many people as possible to start taking notice of the wonderful creatures around them.

BRIAN E. SMALL is a full-time professional bird and nature photographer. For more than 30 years, he has traveled widely across North America to capture images of birds in their native habitats. He served as the photo editor for *Birding* magazine for 15 years. Small grew up in Los Angeles, graduated from U.C.L.A. in 1982, and still lives there today with his wife Ana, daughter Nicole, and son Tyler.

SPECIES INDEX

B

Blackbird, Red-winged 82
Bluebird, Eastern 57
Bobolink 86
Bunting
    Indigo 128
    Painted 130

C

Cardinal, Northern 122
Catbird, Gray 53
Chickadee
    Black-capped 36
    Carolina 37
Cowbird, Brown-headed 84
Creeper, Brown 38
Crow, American 32

D

Dove
    Eurasian Collared- 9
    Mourning 8

F

Finch
    House 62
    Purple 64
Flicker, Northern 18
Flycatcher, Great Crested 28

G

Goldfinch, American 66
Grackle
    Boat-tailed 88
    Common 87
Grosbeak
    Blue 126
    Evening 69
Grosbeak, Rose-breasted 124

H

Hawk
    Cooper's 14
    Sharp-shinned 16
Hummingbird, Ruby-throated 12

J

Jay, Blue 34
Junco, Dark-eyed 81

K

Kingbird, Eastern 25
Kinglet
    Golden-crowned 47
    Ruby-crowned 46

M

Martin, Purple 44
Meadowlark, Eastern 90
Mockingbird, Northern 52

N

Nuthatch
    Brown-headed 41
    Red-breasted 39
    White-breasted 40

O

Oriole
  Baltimore 91
  Orchard 92

P

Parula, Northern 103
Phoebe, Eastern 27
Pigeon, Rock 10

R

Raven, Common 33
Redpoll, Common 68
Redstart, American 106
Robin, American 56

S

Sapsucker, Yellow-bellied 23
Siskin, Pine 70
Sparrow
  American Tree 75
  Chipping 72
  Field 74
  Fox 78
  House 60
  Savannah 71
  Song 79

White-crowned 76
White-throated 77
Starling, European 51
Swallow
  Barn 42
  Tree 43
Swift, Chimney 11

T

Tanager
  Scarlet 120
  Summer 118
Thrasher, Brown 54
Thrush
  Hermit 59
  Wood 58
Titmouse, Tufted 35
Towhee, Eastern 80

V

Vireo
  Blue-headed 29
  Red-eyed 31
  White-eyed 30

W

Warbler
  Black-and-white 105

Black-throated Green 113
Blackburnian 116
Chestnut-sided 110
Magnolia 108
Orange-crowned 102
Pine 96
Prairie 114
Prothonatory 112
Yellow 98
Yellow-rumped 94
Yellow-throated 104
Waxwing, Cedar 55
Wood-pewee, Eastern 26
Woodpecker
  Downy 20
  Hairy 21
  Pileated 24
  Red-bellied 22
  Red-headed 19
Wren
  Carolina 50
  House 49
  Winter 48

Y

Yellowthroat, Common 100

Goodbye
and good
birding!